MR
HENDRIX
AND THE HOUSE THAT TALKED

Hendrix the Pomeranian puppy's adventures always started on a Monday morning after his owner Olivia had left for work.

Hendrix watched through the window as Olivia got into her red car.

"Bye Bye Olivia," he woofed.

"Bye Bye Olivia," said the green front door with the shiny black letterbox.

Olivia always left Hendrix a handful of treats next to his water bowl.

Hendrix counted how many she had left today.

1 2 3 4 5............

"Sssssssssssssssix"

Sid the Snake slithered up behind Hendrix.

Sid was not a real snake, he lived in front of the door to stop the cold air coming in.

Olivia made him out of different coloured materials.
Sid was Red, Blue, Green, Yellow and Purple.

"Bonjour 'endrix," said Kitty the Toy Cat. "You are looking very 'andsome this morning."
Hendrix blushed.

Kitty was French and her white fur was always clean and brushed.
She wore a beautiful diamond collar around her neck.

Hendrix liked Kitty.
Sid the Snake and Kitty the Cat were Hendrix's best friends.

"What shall we do today 'endrix?" asked Kitty.

"Follow me," woofed Hendrix, as he jumped onto the big, brown, squashy chair.

Kitty and Sid quickly followed.

"Get………..Off………Me," boomed the chair.

Hendrix's fur stood on end as the big, squashy chair threw them all into the air.

"Wheeeeeeeeeeeeeeeeeeeeeeeeee, this is fun," yelped Hendrix, as he somersaulted to the floor.

Hendrix and Sid the snake jumped, ran and slithered across the room,and then raced up the stairs and squeezed under the bed in the spare room.

"This is fun," gasped Hendrix.

"Sssssssssssssssssssssure is," hisses Sid the Snake.

Suddenly Hendrix noticed Kitty was not with them.

He looked left. Then he looked right. Then he looked behind him.

Kitty was nowhere to be seen.

"Where's Kitty?" he asked Sid.

"I don't know," hissed Sid, as they both crawled out from under the bed.

"Kitty where are you?" woofed Hendrix.
"Oh 'endrix I am 'ere please 'elp me."
Hendrix could hear Kitty but he could not see her.
He looked all around the room.
He asked the television if he had seen her. "No. I am switched off, I cannot see anything," replied the television.
He asked the curtains but they just swished "Nooooooooooooooooo."
"endrix, I am 'ere in ze waste paper basket. I cannot get out."

Hendrix raced across the room to the big, shiny waste paper basket.

He was too small to see inside but he could hear Kitty calling him.
"Hang on Kitty I'll get you out."

Then Hendrix pushed and rocked the waste paper basket.
It was very hard work but Hendrix did not care.
He had to rescue Kitty.

Suddenly the basket tipped over and Kitty fell out in a heap of rolled up paper.
"Are you ok?" woofed Hendrix.

Kitty stood up and shook out her beautiful white fur.
"Oh 'endrix you are my 'ero."

Hendrix blushed. He suddenly felt very tired so he went to lie down in his bed and fell fast asleep.

Hendrix was woken up by the green front door with the shiny black letterbox, which said "Olivia is home."

But Hendrix was too tired from his adventures to get up.

"Goodness me," said Olivia.

"You lazy boy, have you been asleep all day?

Come on, up you get, you need a good brisk walk in the park."

Hendrix sighed.

MR HENDRIX

Can you help Mr Hendrix count all his treats?

MR HENDRIX

Help Mr Hendrix find his way through the maze to rescue Kitty

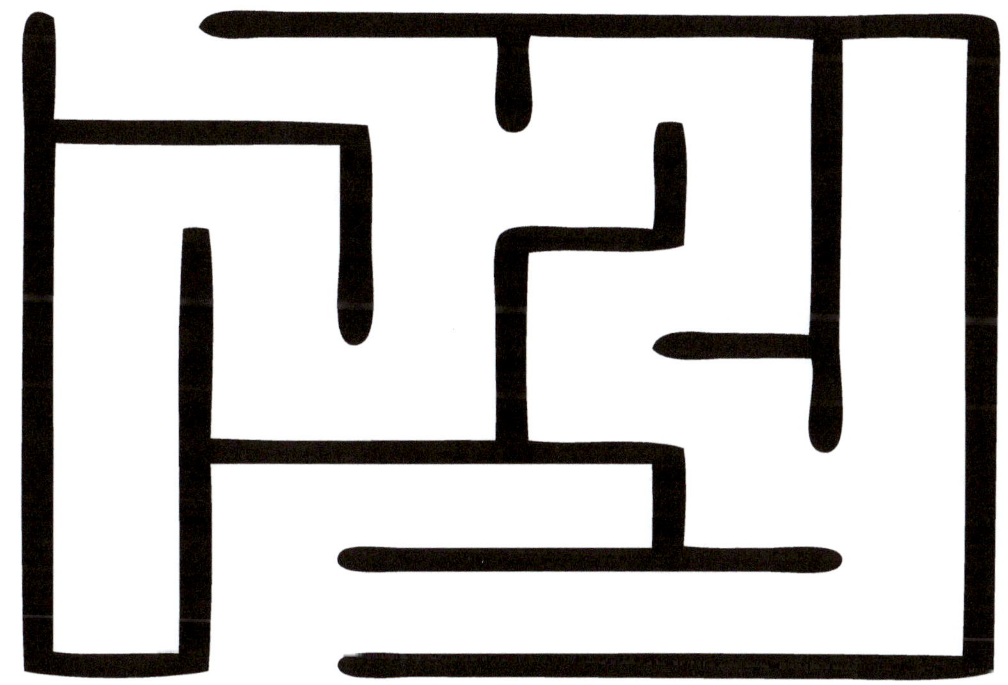

MR HENDRIX

Can you colour in this picture for Mr Hendrix?

MR HENDRIX

Can you colour in this picture for Mr Hendrix?